My Memoir
My Recipe for My Successful Marriage/
How I Turned Turmoil into Triumph

The Self-Published Book of How My Marriage
Became Successful

CAROL F. KIRKENDOLL

My Memoir

My Recipe for My Successful Marriage/How I Turned Turmoil into Triumph

Printed in the United States of America

ISBN: 978-0-578-32903-1

DEDICATION

I dedicate this book to the three loves of my life, my husband, Matthew Kirkendoll Sr., my two sons, Marcus Aceson Ayers, and Mitchel Guy Kirkendoll. Thank you for allowing me to tell my story while including you.

I dedicate this book to all of the readers on their journey to having a successful marriage/relationship.

I dedicate this book to those starting a new relationship and seeking some tools and guidance to hopefully create a successful, long-lasting relationship.

I dedicate this book to all who are hesitant about having a relationship because they believe that it will not happen.

I dedicate this book to those that have loved and lost love and don't believe that you will ever find it again.

I dedicate this book to anyone who has gone through or currently going through hardships in their relationship and doesn't know where to turn.

And lastly, I dedicate this book to those who think there isn't love after difficulty and divorce.

Know that if you can envision it, you can create it.

ACKNOWLEDGEMENT

First and foremost, I need to acknowledge my Lord and Savior, Jesus Christ, for giving me the strength, mindset, and patience to write this book. This book is based on the events of my life and the struggles and growth that I endured during both my marriages. It is written to hopefully help, encourage and motivate others to fight for their relationship and not give up or give in to obstacles that may present while on their journey to success.

I need to acknowledge my husband, Matthew Kirkendoll Sr., for his love, support, and encouragement while writing my memoir. Weathering the storms with me during our 23-year marriage, with a total of 27 years together, and after overcoming all the obstacles that tried to hinder us from moving forward, you are still my rock and love.

My two sons, Marcus and Mitchel, for your support and always believing in me and holding me in your best regards.

I must mention these very special people Anthony B. Ross Sr. and Dr. Linda R. Ross, Ph.D., Connell Page and Sonia Page, Deonte Powell and Ayanna Powell, and Bestman Efejuku and Valentina Efejuku for all your love, support, and participation.

I would like to acknowledge and thank Dennard Mitchell my writing coach and mentor for making my dream a reality, and for all of your knowledge, expertise and genuine support.

To my mother, Verdell Barnes, for allowing me to share a snapshot of your past in my book without judgment. I am extremely grateful for all the support I have received from all my family and friends while on my journey to tell my story.

I have come to the conclusion that not every marriage will survive. Still, with love, patience, and the willingness to work hard for the marriage, you have a fighting chance.

God bless every hand that touches this book. May the words that are imprinted inside help provide the tools and lessons needed to sustain what you have put together.

"What therefore God hath joined together, let not man put asunder." Mark 10:9 KJV,

FOREWORD

When Carol asked me to write the foreword for her new book, I was honored to encourage readers about the value of this literary effort. I am a retired businessman and university professor with experience in accounting, management, marketing, production, and education. Yet, I am drawn to the real-life content of this book because of my own personal experiences in marriage and in raising children with my life partner, my wife. This book illustrates that there are struggles that we can learn from in our lives and from the lives of other people.

I first met Carol more than forty years ago, when her sister, Linda, and I were married. At that time, she was barely a teenager. My exposure to her and the extended family can be characterized as loving and having close family ties. I have watched her conduct in relationships in an episodic way over the years. Now, she is in a very good spot in her life, with a loving husband, Matt. But that was not by accident. The beauty of this book is that it offers folks an opportunity to learn from her experiences in a funny and thoughtful way.

I want to encourage everyone that picks up this book to be blessed, based on the vicarious experience of Carol's exposition of her life's lessons. Readers will be able to avoid and respond to the pitfalls that Carol writes about. Readers will also be shown how to build a bridge to a fulfilling marriage or life partnership.

Anthony B Ross, Sr

MBA, MAFM, CPA, CGMA, CFE, CIA

Core-Life Coaching, LLC

Free 30-Minute
Life Coaching Session

I would like to offer you a free 30-minute Life Coaching Session for purchasing my book.

Thank you for your support.

TO ACCESS, GO TO:

core-lifecoaching.com

When a task is once begun, never leave it till it's done, be the labor great or small, do it well or not at all.

-Author is unknown

"You have to be Brave, You have to be Strong, You have to be courageous."

James Joseph Barnes Sr.

INTRODUCTION

Hello, my name is Carol Kirkendoll. I am a Certified Life Coach, a wife, a mother, and an author. I write this book for all married couples, people in a relationship, and those starting a new relationship who are curious about how to maintain longevity, contentment and have years of success.

I will tie marriage, abuse, and repeated patterns together. I will share life lessons and the tools I have learned through the years to maintain a successful marriage. I will take you through my life journey to show you some of my mistakes in my first and second marriages. Yes, I married twice; hence, I am writing this book to help you avoid the same mistakes I made and hopefully help you have a successful, long-lasting, healthy relationship.

Making the right decisions doesn't always feel good, but it will help you to define what is good for you in your relationship. Hopefully, this book will give you a better understanding that just because there are obstacles in your path doesn't mean you can't continue to move forward as a couple and have a long, loving, healthy marriage.

When I sat down to write this book, I thought of all the couples who threw in the towel prematurely, those who allowed the red flags to cloud their judgment and misguide them on their journey. I found the recipe that helped me and my husband go through the ups and downs and be able to take ownership and continue to love and have a successful marriage.

Marriage is a union between two people, and I believe that anyone can have a successful marriage while going through the learning phase. It will take time and patience, but with the love you share and the willingness to fight for your marriage no matter what, and with great communication and faith, you can survive.

I hope you will read this book without judgment or criticism, but allow me to share my recipe and take you on my journey, which led to my successful marriage.

My hope is that you will find your recipe.

"We told ourselves we had forever and we never looked back. The problem was that we never really looked ahead."

-Crystal Woods

TABLE OF CONTENTS

CHAPTER 1
THE BEGINNING/YOUNG AND NAIVE

Growing up as a young girl in the 1960s, with a large family—six girls and three boys; I had eight siblings. My childhood was very good, and I never gave marriage any thought; it wasn't on my radar. However, I did see what abuse looked like at an early age, although I was too young to understand it. My father was an alcoholic who came home drunk almost every night, and although he never physically harmed my mother, he verbally abused her. He would tear parts of the house up, only to repair it the next day.

At the age of five, I remember one day my father came home drunk, and my brother and I hid behind the couch because we knew he would be drunk. My father served in the Korean war and suffered from what is now called PTSD; he turned to alcohol to cope with and fight his demons.

Outside of his drinking, my father was a very good man; he was hard-working and a great provider. Unfortunately, I would only have him in my life for a short time, as my father died in 1968 in a terrible car accident.

The memory of my father's passing will forever be etched in my mind. Two guys came to the door dressed in police uniforms with shiny black shoes. I was six years old at the time, and I was there when my mother received them at the door. The two guys told my mother that my father was in a terrible car accident. One day he was there and then gone the next. I still have fond memories of my father and how he worked so hard to provide for his family to ensure that his children and wife were well provided for. I remember he would put me on his neck and bounce me around, and he had a love for Jamaican music.

Losing my father at a young age and growing up without my father greatly impacted my life. I didn't realize this until I got older and saw some of the mistakes that I made, which were caused by not having the guidance of a male father figure. I longed to have my father. It was a void in my life, and I would imagine having him there and what it would have been like to have him in my life growing up. I was somewhat envious of my friends who had their fathers in their lives. I now know that some of the choices I made are because I had that part missing.

All the time, my father would tell all his children, "You have to be brave; you have to be strong; you have to be courageous." Those words never left me.

My mother raised nine children all on her own, but we never went without anything in our lives, and she never remarried. After my father passed away, my mother decided to go back to school and take up a trade to help provide for our family. She taught me to be strong and independent and not wait on others to get what I needed but to get it myself. I learned a great deal from my older sisters, as I would watch and listen to them, which kept me from having to experience certain things in life.

At age 13, I decided that I wanted to join a Pentecostal church. I got permission from my mother to join the church. The church was very strict, and it dictated my life while I was a member. However, being a church member helped keep me off the streets and away from doing the things teenagers do during their teenage years, and I always count my blessings for that. During this time in my life, I decided that I would do everything within my power to make sure I never gave my mother any problems. I felt this way because she had so many children to take care of by herself, and I needed to make sure that she didn't have to worry about me. I still try to live my life this way, to this very day, because I feel that if I do the things that I am supposed to do, things will work out great for me, but I've learned that is not always the case.

In 1982, I met my first real boyfriend at a job that we both worked at. I was 19 years old, and marriage was still not a factor because I was too young; however, I didn't know at the time that he would become my husband.

As I began dating my new boyfriend, I battled with whether to leave the church or stay in the church. This decision was a struggle for me, and it was one of the first major decisions I made on my own. I loved attending the church, but it had its struggles, and I had a new boyfriend and wanted to live my life with fewer restrictions. Once the relationship became serious, I decided to leave the church. We worked at a retirement home in Palo Alto, California, where I was a waitress and he in the maintenance department. I was timid and introverted, and he was outgoing. At first, I couldn't believe that I had found someone like him; I was thrilled and excited to have a real boyfriend. He was two years older than I, and he was well advanced in the world and popular while I was very green and hadn't done much in life at that time.

At the beginning of the relationship, we had a lot

of fun together. We shared a love for dancing, and we would go dancing often and to the drive-in movies. We both had a lot of friends, and we shared a lot of common interests. However, I found out years later into the relationship that he was engaging in sexual activities with other females while dating me. I remember a co-worker telling me that he would always say that another coworker would be his next girlfriend. I was hurt by hearing that. I was too naive to understand how to deal with that type of behavior and how critical this was to the relationship; I was under his control. I also didn't comprehend that this would be the beginning of a tumultuous relationship. He had several affairs over the next few years, but I didn't have the tools I needed to address this with him nor the courage. I didn't know how to stand up or speak up; I had no voice and was too shy and naive.

I just went on with the relationship and swept everything under the rug. I didn't know that not addressing this with my boyfriend would only make things more intense. Finally, at the age of 21, I began maturing and becoming a woman and understanding some of the actions in the relationship were not healthy. One year while visiting his family in Memphis, Tennessee, his sister told me he was verbally abusing me. I didn't notice the signs; hell, I didn't even know what verbal abuse was.

I continued in the relationship for several more years. At the age of 25, I decided to get out of the relationship and pursue living my life without him. He and I broke up, and I began dating other men and traveling, doing the things that I enjoyed doing.

In 1986 I started dating a guy in the military. I loved this guy and thought I would have a future with him, but that would not be the case.

The relationship with the guy in the military was short-lived, it ended in 1989, and I headed right back into my old relationship, you know, the abusive, dysfunctional one; without talking or discussing anything, the relationship picked right back up where it left off three years prior. I knew that going back into that relationship wasn't going to work, but I went back where it was familiar. We didn't have anything in common anymore, we barely talked, he hung out with his friends, and I hung out with my friends and family. We didn't know how to be a couple, and I don't think we even tried to be a couple. I would go out and party and drink because I was drowning my sorrows, and I would come home late at night, and he would come home late, and he would be intoxicated most of the time. But we held on to each other because neither one of us wanted to end the relationship or even knew how to end it.

I knew that neither of us was in love, but we had

a love for each other. We carried on as if the past few years didn't exist. Then the unthinkable happened, I got pregnant, the dynamics of the relationship changed drastically. I started focusing on having a baby, and he started focusing on drinking. His behavior became unexplainable. I didn't recognize this guy and why he would turn to alcohol when we should have been rejoicing and celebrating the pregnancy. He was afraid of the unknown and feared being a father. I, too, was afraid. But, on the other hand, I was very excited, and I started making some positive changes in my life and getting my mindset on becoming a mother and getting things ready to bring our new baby home.

During my pregnancy, the relationship took a turn for the worse, and we began arguing and disagreeing about everything. I recall having an altercation one time where I called the police because my boyfriend pushed me, and I was pregnant. But once the police arrived, I hid my belly (True Story). I used to think about that incident years later in disbelief and say to myself. "Did I really do that?" I didn't want him to go to jail, but when I think about it now, I was enabling him.

Finally, when I delivered our son on May 5, 1990, we named him Marcus Aceson; we were both happy about having a new baby boy and building a family with the three of us. I wanted more for my son. I was working at the retirement home, but that wasn't good enough for me to be bringing a child into the world. I decided to go to school to become a medical assistant. My boyfriend would watch the baby during the day while I went to school, and he worked at night at a hospital. After completing the program, I landed a very good job; life was good for the three of us. We were in a pretty good place financially and the relationship was stable.

I started feeling guilty about having a child and not being married; I wanted my son to have both of his parents in his life as a married couple, so I came up with the bright idea right out of the blue, "Let's get married," I know it is hard to believe, but I said those words.

There was no proposal, he agreed, and I started planning a wedding, and in April 1992, I married my first husband. We had a few good years, and he was a good father, but the relationship started to deteriorate not long after the marriage, the fighting started again, and his drinking got worse; we had a few altercations where I called the police, but nothing ever happened. I remember another incident that we had, and I believe that I hit him, and he turned around and hit me in my eye, giving me a black eye; I was in total disbelief that he would hit me as if he didn't care at all, that showed me that he didn't care. The respect level for both of us had diminished, and there was no longer any respect between us. I learned a good lesson that day; Never put my hands on anyone because they just might put theirs on you. I went back to my mother's house for a while, but eventually, I went back to him. All the signs that this relationship was wrong, toxic, unhealthy, and downright dysfunctional were there, but yet I stayed in this relationship before we got married and after the marriage for a total of 13 years until 1994. We were very young when we first met, and it wasn't until years later that I realized how long we had been together.

One night in June of 1994, we had a horrible argument, which led to my husband physically assaulting me. He put his hands around my throat and lifted me off the ground; I was furious and fed up with his behavior that I got a kitchen knife, and I poked him in his left shoulder.

Although I was furious and disgusted, I don't advise anyone to resort to violence of any kind. If you can, please save yourself a lot of heartache and pain by walking away and letting law enforcement handle it; it's not worth the trouble. But, yes, I got myself into a situation with the law, and I ended up having to get a lawyer to defend me for defending myself.

I had to pay fines, do some therapy and community

services while going through my brush with the law, my self-esteem hit rock bottom.

I had so many emotions going on, and I couldn't concentrate on anything besides how I felt about what had transpired between my husband and me. I didn't quite know how to make myself feel good, so I tore myself apart with my negative thoughts, i.e., "I bet you she never got into trouble." "I am a failure" these are the thoughts that stayed in my mind constantly; I was a mess.

I have never been the type of person to burden other people with my problems, so I kept all my problems to myself and continued with my life. It was hard, but I had to stay focused on my son and keep him safe.

I had court-ordered therapy, and for the first two weeks of therapy, I just cried, and the therapist allowed me to do so. I couldn't get any words out, felt like a failure, and had very low self-esteem.

I couldn't even believe that I allowed myself to get in trouble with the law. I went through a lot because of what I did; it took me about three years to be free of all the things I had to do to put that incident behind me.

*"Something good comes out of
every crisis."*

-Dave Pelzer

Chapter 2
THERAPY AND DECISIONS

As a result of having a brush with the law in 1994, I discovered therapy, and let me tell you, it was one of the best things that have ever happened to me. Being able to talk and let go of all of those negative emotions was freeing. It was as if I was finding myself, a person I never knew existed; however, I still had low self-esteem, and I was ashamed of myself, and I carried that burden with me for many, many years.

I struggled with "should I leave the marriage, or should I stay in the marriage?" Just like I did when I decided to leave the church that I was attending years back. Now I was faced with another huge decision to make in my life.

I even called my mother-in-law in Tennessee to let her know that I had decided to end the marriage. She was very supportive of my leaving because years before, she knew what his sister had told me about him verbally abusing me. Let me tell you, I thought making the decision to leave the church was a hard decision but leaving and ending my marriage was the hardest thing I had to do.

After coming to terms with me ending the marriage, I knew that I had to get my son and me out of that toxic situation. So, in September of 1994, I decided to take a trip to Arizona to visit one of my older sisters. When I arrived in Arizona, it was the monsoon season—the ground was wet; it had sprinkles of rain coming down, and it was hot and humid.

My sister took me around the city of Gilbert, where she lived, and it was simply beautiful and new. I was in awe; I immediately decided that I wanted to move there with my son and just start over fresh. I was excited and was getting a plan into place, trying to figure out what I needed to do to move from California to Arizona.

Several months went by, and I was still going through therapy and finishing up all of the court-ordered things I needed to do before I could move. I was still in the marriage, trying to figure out what I wanted to do about moving to Arizona or what exactly to do with my life. I now know that in relationships, I can't give what I don't have.

I filed for divorce in 1994, but that came with a huge price. I needed a lawyer to assist me with the divorce and receiving child support; the process was long and drawn out. I would go to court time and time again, and my husband would never show up for court dates. One day in January 1995, the judge asked me if I wanted to continue to wait to see if my husband would show up. I told him no and that I didn't have enough money to continue to pay my lawyer. At that time, the judge asked me if I wanted to be divorced that day, and I said, "yes, sir." Then, immediately, he granted me a divorce.

The judge proceeded to ask me about child support for our son, and I told the judge that I asked my husband if he would pay me $300.00 a month. The judge asked, "what did he say?" I told him that he said no, at that moment (I remember those words very clearly to this day). The judge said, "he told you no?" And I said, "yes, sir." He looked at his paperwork which was my husband's income information, and then the judge looked at me and said, "okay, then he will pay you $600.00 a month." I was so happy. It was a very good day to have gotten a divorce and a child support settlement all in the same day.

My ex-husband wasn't happy that he had to pay

me double what I originally asked for, and he had child support for many years. He fell behind a few times, but I would receive checks on a regular basis. I recommend that every parent who is the sole provider seek child support to help raise their children.

After the divorce was finalized, I would receive the money to help raise my son, which helped a lot. However, I still had a cloud over my head because I was faced with even lower self-esteem because now, I am a divorcee and a single mother.

My thoughts did a number on me. Not only did I divorce my husband, I left my son's father, but I knew we couldn't stay in that toxic situation. My thoughts of how my father was not in my life and how I grew up without my father lingered in my mind because that was the very reason why I decided to get married so my son could have both his parents in his life. I also thought about how my mother stayed in that toxic relationship but, back in the 1960s, divorce wasn't very popular and wasn't really heard of; besides, she loved my father.

While still going through my process with therapy, I was moved to a women's group session because I had made such good progress in my one-on-one sessions my therapist felt like it was a good time to move me into a group setting. There I saw that I wasn't alone and that other women had gone through similar situations like mine, and I didn't feel so bad anymore. I actually felt empowered that other women had made mistakes just like I had and were turning their lives around. I learned a great deal of coping techniques, like how to deal with stress and how to know the signs of any type of abuse, whether it is mental or physical. I also learned how to address it without violence.

I decided to take back my power and redesign myself, hold my head up and not walk in shame anymore, and be the mother my son deserved. I later realized that it was because of my son that I made the final decision to leave his father as that was not the life that I envisioned for my son and me. I believe that therapy saved my life. It was very therapeutic, and I would never be ashamed of going to therapy to take care of myself. Therapy was something that was much needed for me. After all the sessions were completed, I didn't want to leave the women that I became so close to. I decided to wait until my son got a little older before I put him in therapy, although I later wished I had done it sooner to help him go through the process.

I will always give all glory and honor to God for the lessons I've learned during my time in therapy. A huge takeaway from getting therapy is that it showed me how broken I was, how angry I was, and by receiving therapy, it showed me myself. I am a firm believer in therapy and how it helped me to see the role I played in the marriage. It helped me heal and not hold on to past experiences and life lessons. I'm not saying that I have forgotten the things I've gone through but what I am saying is that I don't allow my past experience to dictate how my life is going to go.

After attending therapy, I knew that I was growing, healing and making progress when I could talk about my bad experience. It took me many years to even mention what had taken place and all the things I had to go through. It wasn't that I was embarrassed; I just didn't know how to bring it up or talk about it. I knew that I didn't want to stuff it down and move forward. With time and growth, I was not shocked by it anymore, and I came out of it still standing. I also saw an opportunity to help others that have gone through a bad time in their life. I remember having to call my manager to let her know what had happened and what she told me still sticks with me to this day; it was what I needed to hear at that moment. She said to me, "This too shall pass." I believe I cried because of the support she showed me and that she never judged me. I want to believe with therapy, I was able to get to this place in my life.

A lot of people believe that going to therapy is a sign of weakness and is embarrassing, but it's quite the opposite. While I was going through therapy, I had a nonjudgmental/unbiased person sitting in front of me, listening to me. She was ready and willing to help me with no judgment whatsoever. What I can suggest is, don't rule out therapy and deny yourself the opportunity to heal and become a better version of yourself. Imagine if I had never gone through therapy, how broken I would have remained, and I probably would have kept going back into that toxic marital relationship.

If you feel you need therapy, don't be ashamed to get it. If you allow therapy to help you heal by doing the work, you will most likely see its value. If you are in a relationship and your partner doesn't want to go, you go and take care of yourself; that's exactly what I did.

My thoughts regarding therapy are that you can't go wrong. Hopefully, during the process, it will help you heal from the inside out; it can help you have hope again. So many people are stuck in toxic relationships with no way out and no one to turn to, so they go on, year after year, leaving things the way they are.

I must mention an update: In January 2012, I received a phone call from my ex-husband out of the blue, and he told me that he was not going to pay me any more money, and from that time, I haven't received any money from him. I still have an open child support case on him, and our son is 31 years old. In July of 2020, I received a check from DES; I believe it was a stimulus check and then no money since then. I will always leave the child support case open because I raised my son, and I am hoping to get the rest of the child support that is still pending.

"Where there is love there is life."

-Mahatma Gandhi

CHAPTER.3
THE GAME-CHANGER

O ne Friday night in March of 1994, my sisters, a friend, and I decided to go out dancing. We went to the Stardust lounge in Sunnyvale, California, the "kick-it spot," a tiny hole in the wall but popular nonetheless. While I stood, enjoying my cocktail, a group of guys walked into the club, and they caught my eye, and I looked; I immediately said, "Kirkendoll." I knew who one of the guys was, and boy did the game change at the moment, and so did my life, that night was magical, and I was on cloud nine.

It was Matthew Kirkendoll; we knew each other as children, as his family lived down the street from my cousins. When I would see him, I would go into the house because I was a very shy little girl and wasn't into boys at that age. Matthew was very close with my brothers. They hung out together for many years. He would ask my brothers about me, and my brother would tell Matthew, "My sister is a good girl; leave her alone." I still laugh when he tells that story.

One particular day while I was visiting my mother, I met Matthew and a friend working on a car. He told his friend, "If I could get with that young lady right there, I would change my whole life around." and he was a man of his word. After seeing him in the club, Matthew and I talked and danced and had a great night. He tried to get me to go to the after-the-club event, but I humbly declined, after which he went his way, and I went mine.

During the time I became reacquainted with Matthew, I didn't see him for a very long time. While the drama in my first marriage was taking place, I kept moving forward in the midst of it. I didn't plan on dating anyone; I focused on taking care of my son and myself. Fate would have it that Matthew and I would run into each other again at the same club, and then he and I formed a friendship over time.

I was, at this time, still deciding whether to leave my husband, going to therapy, and nursing very low self-esteem. Matthew was very friendly and a gentleman; he played his position with poise and patience. After meeting Matthew, I knew that I needed to get out of the toxic marital relationship with my then-husband. I remember something Matthew said to me. "If anything should transpire between you and me, it would be you making the first move." He meant that he wanted to make sure that I didn't feel pressured by him, and I really respected that. One afternoon Matthew came over to my mother's home, and I just so happened to be there; (I suspect he came by to see if my car was there). We started talking, and we decided to grab a bite to eat. It was our first time hanging out together; to keep it platonic, we decided to go Dutch (to split the bill). We talked, and I explained to him my situation with my husband; I told him I was married and was in the process of ending the marriage and that I had a son. It was a lovely time for both of us.

Matthew and I became friends quickly, we would talk about everything, and we quickly grew fond of each other. Matthew came into my life when I needed someone to talk to, a shoulder to cry on, and he would ride with me to my therapy sessions and wait until they were over. The friendship was unexplainable at that time. I remember the feeling that I felt with Matthew, it was fresh and brand new, and I hadn't felt this way for many years. It is almost unexplainable how this man made me feel after coming out of a long dysfunctional relationship.

I had spent 13 years in a toxic relationship, and to have someone so compassionate, nice, and attentive to me was a great feeling. Ending my marriage started weighing heavy on my mind, and I knew that I needed to make a final decision to end the marriage. It was so hard and painful, mixed with being scary.

I recall the day I decided to talk with my then-husband and let him know I wanted a divorce. I knew that I needed to have this talk with him, and I knew that it would be painful for the both of us; this wasn't easy. I asked him to meet me at my mother's house so that he and I could speak because we were separated and no longer living together. So, he met me there, and we sat outside of my mother's house in his car, and I told him that I wanted a divorce. He listened and was very quiet, he didn't get mad, he wasn't violent, and we had a nice talk. At that moment, I had so many mixed emotions. I was relieved and sad all at the same time. That, too, was an unfortunate time for the both of us, but I knew the marriage was over, and I wanted to end it on a positive note and not blindside him. This was no easy task by any means, but it needed to be done. What I took away from that moment was that I didn't have to be vindictive or conniving; I just needed to tell my truth; I felt good about how I handled it.

I knew that divorcing would be challenging and painful, and it doesn't matter if you are the person initiating the divorce or not; it sucks. But, concluding that I needed to divorce, it came with a price, mentally, physically, emotionally, and financially. I don't believe that all divorces are nasty; I know that some are mutual and amicable. On the other hand, some divorces are downright brutal, and that's what I didn't want. I wanted to end the relationship as peacefully as possible. Where I believe I went wrong was not talking with our son to let him know that Mommy and Daddy love you, and this has nothing to do with you. I battled with this for many years.

During the separation, my then-husband would pick our son up on the weekend to spend time with him, but that all came to a screeching halt because, on one particular Saturday in 1995, my then-husband picked our son up for a visit, and we just so happened to be headed in the same direction. Unfortunately, he saw me riding in the car with Matthew, and he was livid. Later he told me that he wasn't going to pick up our son so I could hang out with other guys (and that's putting it nicely). That day was the last visit he had with our son. Marcus's father stopped the visitation, which was devastating for our son and me. I felt horrible. I felt like I caused all of this because I decided to end the marriage, and my son paid the ultimate price; he didn't have his father in his life anymore.

It reminded me of losing my father at a young age and its effects on me; I was around the same age when I lost my father. It seemed as if my then-husband didn't care about seeing our son. He just wanted to hurt me, but my son paid the price. I tried to get him to come around and pick up our son, but he literally walked out of his life and returned to Tennessee without notifying us about his move.

I felt as if I had created a big mess, and I blamed myself for what had transpired. I wanted to fix it, but there wasn't anything I could do but try and pick the pieces for my son.

One thing I will say is when you're faced with a decision like I was, please think about the moves you want to make before you make them. Look at the situation from every angle and consider the possible consequences and how they could affect others before making a final decision. Make sure the timing is right for you and everyone involved.

During this time in my life, I had a good friend in Matthew, and he never overstepped his boundaries with me. He sympathized with the things that I had to deal with in my first marriage and was always there to support my son and me.

Before living on my own, my son and I stayed a short time with a friend and with my younger sister until I decided it was time to find a place for my son and me, so I found an apartment. While at work one day, Matthew came to my job and gave me a few hundred dollars to help me get on my feet and pay for the apartment, and I was very shocked and thrilled by his kindness.

When it was time for my son and me to move, Matthew took some time off from work to help me move into my new apartment. I knew that I liked him and saw exactly where our relationship was headed. When I met Matthew, everyone thought this would be a fling and wouldn't last. No one took us seriously at this point. Still, Matthew and I saw our relationship as a long-term relationship, and I knew from the moment I saw him in the club that this would be something real.

Matthew would help me financially, and he would go with me to therapy sessions and wait in the car for me. He was with me every step of the way, helping me rebuild my life and becoming a good friend that, in late 1995, he became my new boyfriend. We were a couple and Matthew moved in with Marcus and me. Again, I went on the mission to build a family with the three of us. We did everything together, just the three of us. We had a very beautiful life; we had friends and family in our lives. We would incorporate both our families together by having parties and going to both family houses for the Holidays. By doing that, we could spend time with both Matthew's and my family.

Life was good, and I was feeling very happy in my new relationship with Matthew. We had a really good thing going. About a year later, in 1996, I became pregnant with my second son. I was so happy; words can't explain how happy I was because I was truly in love, and having my love child with the man I love was a great feeling.

I delivered our baby boy on January 31, 1997; we named him Mitchel Guy. Matthew and I were very excited to have another child, and Matthew decided that we needed a bigger place to live in. We moved into a new apartment with two bedrooms so that Marcus and Mitchel would have their own space.

I was very excited about how our life was going and about having a new beginning, but guilt kicked in, and I couldn't control my thoughts. My mind kept racing back to the time during the separation with my ex-husband and how that time should have been a time in my life for my son and me, where we should have spent time together healing and bonding with each other. It was as if my mind wouldn't allow me to be happy.

My thoughts ran rampant through my mind, and it played on and on, almost like a broken record saying, "I started a new relationship, and I didn't sit my son down to have a conversation with him about what was going on in our lives." It was a lot to deal with.

Marcus was five years old during my separation from his father, and he was brilliant at that age, and I know he would have understood what I was explaining to him. (I'm getting very emotional writing this.) I've learned from this experience that I should have considered my son's feelings and waited, but that was not the case, and as I now look at where we are today, everything worked out how it was supposed to.

I want to share something with you:

I was once told by someone that I didn't have to sell my husband; in other words, I don't have to try to make people like him. When I was told this, he and I were very fresh into our relationship and some were on the fence about him. As I write this today and reflect on those words that never left me, I want to take the time to give you some insight into the man that I have been with for 27 years and married to for 23 years and counting.

To know Matthew is to know a man of his word, someone who is loyal and dependable, who loves to help others. When he starts out to do something, he won't stop until he gets it done or accomplishes that goal. Matthew is very supportive of me and all the things that I want to do; he is a very positive person that doesn't allow the hardships of life to get him down. I never see him in a down or depressed state of mind because he's a go-getter. I often sit and wonder how he does it, how he won't allow anything to get him down or to lose faith. He's helped me in ways that no one could ever imagine. When some ask me to help them with something, they can expect my husband to be right there by my side, helping where he can. One trait that I absolutely love about my husband is how much he loves his mother— how he gloats over her and calls her his sweetheart (I'm smiling). This is something that really stood out because I know if he loves and cherishes her, he will love and cherish me; this was truly a game-changer for me.

Some women would probably get mad or jealous if their husband loved his mother the way Matthew loves his, but quite the contrary, I adore it. Some people won't take the time to notice that the love that a man has for his mother is a totally different love from that he has for his wife; I know the difference. There isn't anything that I haven't asked for in my marriage that I haven't received; some would call that "A Kept Woman," but I call it a woman that is truly loved by a man.

There's no need for me to sell him. I know who I married and the kind of man he is, and I have said it before, and I will say it again, he is far from perfect, but he is perfect for me. My life changed for the better when Matthew came into it, we've weathered many storms, but today when I look at where we are and what we went through to get here, I wouldn't change anything. The struggles that Matthew and I endured in our relationship are the very reason I am able to shed the light that every relationship will have problems but, my suggestion to you is, hold on tight and keep moving in the same direction, pray like never before, and don't give up.

"Most often, what I don't know will have a vastly greater bearing on my life more than what I do know."

— Craig D. Lounsbrough

CHAPTER 4
ADDRESSING THE RED FLAGS

In my 13-year relationship with my ex-husband, there were so many red flags that I simply ignored; all the signs were there, but I was too naive to notice. Over the years, I would sit back and reflect on all of the mistakes made on both our part; age and immaturity played a huge factor. But I didn't know how to express myself or speak up for myself; I didn't have a voice, so I never addressed his actions of infidelity.

There was the red flag of excessive drinking, but we both did it, so I felt it was okay until things got out of hand. By then, it was well past having a conversation because we both had created too much damage.

As I mentioned, I didn't know that he was verbally abusing me. I didn't know that he was disrespecting me, nor did I know I was being disrespectful to him. I had to learn about red flags; yes, you know what they are, and here is what I've learned over the years about "Red Flags."

I define Red Flags as those things that keep flying by, waving and saying, "grab me, grab me, grab me, why don't you!" But I was so blinded by lust and whatever I thought was love that I ignored the red flags. I just kept on with life as if everything was okay, only to say years later, "I saw that, I knew that, but I just ignored it."

I now understand what red flags are; they're what I call warning signs. They're like the caution signs that we see on the road that we sometimes ignore, only to find out that the road isn't safe at all. From my experience, hindsight is 20/20. I know we can't turn back the hands of time, but I wish that when I met my first husband, I would have been guarded and cautious. I don't think I should have been an open book at that point; I was so young and naive.

I know now that he and I stopped growing, we stopped believing in each other, and the love just fizzled out, but we kept on moving forward in the relationship. There has to be mutual respect in a marriage, and communication is key; if the communication is off or one-sided, that's a huge red flag.

I met both of my husbands in different stages of my life, and whatever stage I was in my life, that's how I should have approached the relationship. I feel that I didn't know any better. Years later, I saw everything clearly.

With my current husband, I was in a very low state of mind. That's when I should have been very aware and cautious going into a new relationship. I should have been on the lookout for any signs that may have raised my eyebrows. During my low state, I was trying to fill a void and could have been taken advantage of, but that wasn't the case for me with Matthew because the relationship worked out.

As I stated, I kept asking myself, are you looking to fill that void? Are you rushing into a new relationship, ignoring all the warning signs (red flags)?

In my opinion, a person with low self-esteem shouldn't be looking for anyone at that point; they should be seeking help to work through their issues; that is a big red flag and should be addressed immediately. I now know that I was going through my healing process, and I wasn't completely whole.

There were times I felt like I was bringing all my baggage from the previous relationship into the new relationship because I would sometimes feel angry, bitter, and broken. I was present in the new relationship but not all the way healed from the previous one; that's another big red flag. My suggestion to you is to take the time you need to heal and reset and go through whatever process you choose in order to fix what is broken with you mentally. Take the time to be with just you and reconnect with yourself.

At the time, I was wounded and broken, and I had blinders on, and I just couldn't see any of this because I really didn't have the knowledge regarding it. I now know that red flags come in different situations, and when red flags show up and when they are not addressed in a timely manner, they become bigger problems and can get out of control.

I've learned there is a way to address red flags; my suggestion is to ask, "can we talk about that?" I want to make sure I talk to my husband and not at him; yes, there is a difference, like addressing something versus confronting someone. The point of addressing the red flag is to avoid it repeatedly happening with the hopes of resolving any conflict it could cause.

Leaving the red flags unaddressed only to never talk about them, I believe, is a huge mistake often made, and I am guilty of that. I now know that I have to pick my battles, and not every little thing needs addressing, but if that is who you are and how you handle your relationship, then so be it. When I address the red flags early on, it leads to a better relationship with better communication, trust, and honesty. An excellent way I've found that worked in my marriage is knowing my husband and his triggers.

I try to address red flags that occur early on and not wait too long before bringing them up to my husband. I had to learn how to handle and approach the red flag so that I didn't upset my husband or get upset myself. What I do now is wait to see when it is a good time to address the red flag because I've learned how my husband will receive what I am saying.

I don't go in for the kill, but to get some clarity and understand what is going on. I have learned to leave out words that are blaming, "You Always," "You Keep," "You Never," these words are blaming and are pointing a finger only at your mate. I found that using my love language helps calm the situation and helps me better transition into the conversation.

Years into our relationship, I was disrespectful and selfish and really didn't care how I approached situations; these were repeated patterns that I did not want to revisit, only to have the same outcomes. I try to be careful because I know that my husband has feelings, and I may have to ease into the conversation because no matter what my deliverance is, he won't receive it well if I'm not careful and thoughtful.

There may be times when you want to address a

red flag and your mate doesn't want to talk or they may create a situation; that too is a red flag. That is a coping mechanism, where the other person is telling you they don't want to deal with what you are saying, so they create an argument or they completely shut down; that's a huge red flag.

I believe that denial is a red flag; when someone constantly denies something and never takes ownership of their actions, that is a red flag, and this is something that should be addressed.

While addressing red flags, I want to speak on the dating process and some of the things that I have learned over the years about dating and hope it will help others just starting out or starting a new relationship. In my opinion, the dating process is the time in the relationship where two people get to know the other person.

This process should not be rushed; the two should spend as much time as they can talking and asking many questions, sharing and telling each other their likes and dislikes, i.e., do you want children? Yes, how many? No, why not? What are your favorite foods? What are your hobbies? Do you have siblings? Yes. How many? You get the picture.

I had so many missed opportunities while going through the dating process. If I had taken my time and done my homework properly, I would have found out early on in the dating phase in my first marriage that my first husband wasn't the right person for me to date. Getting to know and spending time with the other person is vital. Taking the time to use dating as a first interview, so to speak, and paying attention to the things that he or she is saying or doing, I believe, can save years of heartache and pain. If there are any red flags, they will present themselves, and what you do with them will determine how the relationship will turn out.

With my first marriage, I learned that we should have never rushed the dating process, and we should have handled the dating process with grace, patience, and time. We did the opposite; we skipped through the dating process, ignoring every red flag that came our way, and moved into "I Love You." What a missed opportunity. We could have found out everything we needed to know about each other in the dating phase, but we were in such a rush to get to I love you, we missed all of the red flags.

I now know to look out for a few red flags: a drinking problem, sex addiction, constant lying, cheating /infidelity, drug abuse, and an open relationship. Had me and my husband addressed my low self-esteem, lack of communication, and insecurities, had we both addressed these things, we might have stood a fighting chance.

The signs were all there had we just addressed them. It is my belief that if we had taken the time to get to know each other, we could have ended the relationship way before we went to the altar,

I can only imagine how many relationships would have never taken place if the couple had taken the time to address the red flags or even acknowledged them; maybe they might have seen that this is not the person for me. Can you imagine how many relationships have continued with so many problems throughout their relationship because they chose to ignore the red flags and said, we can work through this only to disagree, fight or end in divorce?

I wish the dating process was mandatory when new relationships are just beginning; we all know that that is not realistic. The dating process is where a soon-to-be or hope-to-be couple can find out so much information about the other person; it pretty much lays the foundation for the relationship. If the couple knew early on in the dating process that the one person doesn't want children and the other party does, this is clearly a red flag that should be addressed immediately, and a decision should be made at that point whether to continue on with the relationship.

Find out about each other's religious values. Maybe he wants to live as a Christian and she wants to live a more lenient life and party; this should be addressed early on. I believe that not all red flags are wrong, some red flags are meant to bring awareness to start a conversation to be addressed, and the two can carry on with the relationship. Some people really think that they will change the other person as time goes by; this is a possibility but, why risk it by taking a chance on what is supposed to be a lifetime? After all, the goal of dating or seeking a relationship is to possibly find a lifelong partner, someone who shares your common interest, someone who's going in the same direction as you, someone to share your dreams with, and someone you can grow old together with.

Sometimes opposites attract, which is where excellent communication comes into play, and you learn how to balance each other out. People can change their relationships because they believe in it and value the relationship, so they change for its betterment. Skipping through the most critical part of the relationship is like setting up for a ticking time bomb because all of those red flags you've let fly by will resurface, I guarantee you that.

Why not address them early on, and avoid them rearing their ugly heads years into the marriage? If the person you are dating tells you that they don't want to get married or do not want children, get clarification on what that means, i.e., find out if they mean never or no time soon, get clarification on exactly what they mean so you can determine if you should continue to date this person. That's called addressing the red flag; if you feel that it is a red flag, then it is one, and the red flags should be addressed immediately.

Learn to listen to what the other person is saying in conversations with you or others; you can learn a great deal of what they want or their likes or dislikes. Try to learn as much as you can about the other person early on so that you can eliminate hardship years down the road.

What's the saying? Hindsight is 20/20. If I only knew all of the things I mentioned above before I entered into both of my marriages, I believe that we wouldn't have had so much turmoil. I now have the necessary tools to understand when a situation needs addressing, when to table the conversation for a later time, or when the conversation can be received without being judgmental, harsh, or biased.

This came with years of experience with my current husband. Having a heart-to-heart conversation about situations that may come up in the relationship only helps to clear up and clarify what is needed or expected to carry on with a healthy relationship.

As a couple, we are forever learning as we go through our relationship, and most of the time, we won't get it right all the time; that's where communication comes in. Holding things in and not asking to have a conversation is a red flag in itself; there is a way to communicate with your mate, using love language, i.e., "I have something on my mind, and I would like to talk with you about it."

During the conversation, try to be courteous by addressing the comments in a way that doesn't cause more conflict. Remember the love language, i.e., you make me feel like this when you say that to me; try using words like, "I heard you say that when I did that to you, you felt angry."

I am a firm believer that talking to your mate can calm down the situation and help both get their feelings out without shouting or arguing with each other. It might sound strange to say that there is a right and wrong way to have a discussion, but every discussion should not turn into an argument. I've learned that when my husband and I disagree and there's shouting, neither one of us is hearing the other, we are just shouting at that point, and nothing is getting solved.

Everyone wants to get their point across and wants to be heard; arguing about a situation means that you disagree. Therefore, during the disagreement, it would be an excellent time to sit and listen to what the other person has to say, try to digest it, and work through it together.

If I may, I want to share one of the big regrets I have

with both of my marriages, which is not getting a proposal. This haunts me often, and it is a huge red flag for me. Some women may disagree with me, and that is their right, but it is my belief that every woman should be proposed to. I believe that it is part of the dating process, and it is the starting point leading into the marriage. My belief is, when the subject of marriage comes up and both parties are in agreement, the proposal phase should begin.

Men, this is my opinion that the proposal is sacred to women and should be well thought out while going through the dating phase. Notice some of the things she likes; if she is an introvert and needs a quiet, intimate proposal or if she is an extravert and needs that attention. Whatever is chosen, please do not eliminate this part of the dating process leading into the engagement; it is very important. Ladies, don't settle, expect it, I didn't, and I am telling you, you will regret it. This still bothers me to this day.

When it comes to the matter of the heart, I believe sometimes people tend to compromise and overlook things with the hope that later on, it will get better or it will change itself. I would never want to see another female lose out on the opportunity of being proposed to or have children or whatever her hopes and dreams are, or a male not getting what his heart desires in a relationship because both failed to have very important conversations about the matter.

Remember, you are creating your recipe for your successful marriage!

"Divorce isn't such a tragedy. A tragedy's staying in an unhappy marriage, teaching your children the wrong things about love. Nobody ever died of divorce."

-Jennifer Weiner

CHAPTER 5
DIVORCE AND MISTAKES

When I used to think of divorce, I would always think of a bad time, a hard time, or a failed marriage. Going through my divorce, I felt like a failure, like I didn't get it right. However, I realized that we were very young, as I mentioned previously, and we didn't have the tools to sustain a marriage.

You would probably look at me crazy if I mentioned words such as "Successful Divorce," yes, it does sound kind of crazy when you say it. When I came to the conclusion that I needed to get a divorce, it was something that needed to be done. In my opinion, all divorces aren't bad; some are amicable while some are downright brutal. For me, divorce changed me and helped me in ways that I never imagined. It helped me see value within myself and helped me get my self-esteem back and find out who I really am.

Divorce can be very painful; it tore me down and left me broken-hearted. Still, after I went through therapy, I was able to get myself together. I saw how getting my son and me out of that toxic marriage made me a stronger person, and it gave my son some peace from all of the fighting we were doing.

I hear many people say, "I'm never getting a divorce," or "I didn't get married to get a divorce," my opinion on that is that I don't think anyone goes into a marriage with divorce on their mind? Life happened, and when the cards were dealt, I played my hand and played to win to the best of my ability.

I believe that sometimes divorce is very much necessary and should happen. I would never try to stay in a marriage just to say I'm married; I don't believe in staying in a marriage because of the children. Divorces take place for many different reasons; only the couple can determine why or when they should go through a divorce.

There are questions I would ask myself over and over again, such as, "Am I staying in this marriage because of my son"? Did I give my marriage my all? Did I exceed every possibility to keep the marriage intact? I believe these are some very important questions that every couple should ask themselves before making a permanent decision.

As I stated before, I made a big mistake not

talking with my son. As the parent, I made all the decisions, but I should have spoken with my son. I wish I had given him the opportunity to know and process what was going on. I've learned a huge lesson, and now I believe that if children are of age and can understand what is going on, they should be told so that they too can process that their parents are divorcing.

Some questions I ask are, "what if the child is angry or grieving the loss of their parents' relationship?" Shouldn't they have an opportunity to speak up and express how they feel? I know that my divorce had an impact on my son.

My son was very close to the age that I was when I lost my father. My son lost his father to divorce, but he lost him nonetheless. My son is a grown man now, and we don't really talk about his father, but I know that he has come to terms with what his father did.

As I stated earlier, all divorces don't have to be brutal. I had a classmate tell me how she told her husband that she wanted a divorce and how they are friends to this day and co-parented their son when he was a child.

I had another friend call me and tell me how her husband left in the middle of the night and didn't have the guts to tell her that he wanted a divorce. Whichever way it happens, divorce is not a pretty thing. I believe the way that the divorce is handled is related to how the outcome will be.

When Matthew and I were going through some tough times, I was told by a pastor that if you didn't hear God say the word divorce, then don't mention it. I've seen some people get divorced prematurely without trying to make the marriage work. The first thing that comes out of their mouths in a disagreement is "Divorce." In my opinion, divorce is very serious and shouldn't be taken lightly. I also believe some divorces are long overdue and should have taken place years ago, and some are dragged out because one party wants to win. Well, let me enlighten you from my experience; no one really wins in a divorce; however, there is life after a divorce.

Another thing I've learned and would love to share is that I should have taken the time to spend more time with myself during the healing process. Here we go, another mistake I made is not taking the time to be with just me and my son. I am over it now, but I spent many years regretting that I didn't take the time to bond with my son and make sure he was okay after the divorce. That should have been the time where my son and I reconnected with each other. I chose to get into a new relationship, as I mentioned before.

As I entered into the new relationship, things

worked out fine, and at that point, I felt blessed. If I could offer any advice to you, please, after ending a relationship, take a breath and collect yourself, get some therapy if needed, reconnect the parts that have been damaged in your life and your children's lives.

I see all of my mistakes clearly now, which is why I can share them with you. Not everyone will go through the same things in their relationships or marriage but understanding what went wrong and learning from that is key. I believe that every relationship is different. Only the couple on the journey together can define what a perfect marriage or relationship looks like.

I feel in my heart of hearts that my marriage is a success because of the years we have and the work that we've put into the marriage. We're still learning because, in life, there's always going to be room for growth. I like to speak from experience that if you see a shift in your marriage and things are not going the way they used to, that's a red flag and not necessarily a negative red flag, but it is enough to spark a conversation.

I also know from experience that couples go through growing pangs; this is the time to sit down and talk. Many couples go years and years without any changes in their marriage. What worked in the early 1990s may not work in the mid-2020s. We tune up our cars, get makeovers and upgrade our wardrobes but let our marriage go to hell in a handbasket.

In my opinion, divorcing can be hard, as I mentioned earlier, but it does not have to be a death sentence, and it doesn't mean you failed as a couple. It simply means that the marriage ran its course, and it is time to move forward with your life.

I would never want to be the star player on a losing team. I now know how important it is to communicate and work things out. Still, if the other party is unwilling to work as a team, I can't see how the relationship can win. Don't be afraid to make mistakes; still, try not to keep making the same mistakes. The key is to learn from your mistakes and do better. I've mentioned time again that communication will help in every situation you may face. Try to work through the hardships as a couple and not go at it alone. My belief is when there are situations that come up, if you both tackle them together, you will most likely have greater outcomes. I had to learn this the hard way. Being supportive regardless of whether you are staying together or not can help to ease the pain.

As I mentioned before, divorce can be devastating, and as crazy as it may sound, having a plan in place is also helpful. Having a full understanding of why the decision to divorce is even being considered is very important. Try to avoid making a huge mistake by acting prematurely and rushing into a permanent decision that may have a long-lasting effect. I can now see the mistakes that I made, which is why I am giving some suggestions to help you navigate through the process of making such a huge decision. I didn't really have anyone to guide me through my process because I kept everything to myself, and it wasn't until I met my Matthew that I had someone to share my journey with.

The struggle is real, and the most important thing you can do is to take care of yourself and if there are children involved, take care of them as well. With time you will begin to heal and you will be able to pick up the pieces and if the decision to stay in the marriage is made, you will start anew and there's where the new journey as a couple will begin.

"True love stories never have endings."

-Richard Bach

CHAPTER 6
LOVE IN FULL BLOOM

Matthew and I had a real love affair. I don't think that anyone thought that Matthew and my relationship would last as long as it has. When we first met in 1994, I believe that both of us needed rescuing, and fate would have it that we found each other during that time.

A great memory I have was when Matthew, my younger sister, Sonia, and a male friend went to San Francisco on a dinner boat cruise; that was a very fun night (*I am smiling while writing this*). The cruise was very fun, we ate good food and drank. Matthew and the male friend didn't drink alcohol, but my sister and I did; we were pretty liquored up and feeling good at that time. On the ride home, I was talking with Matthew, and "I love you" kept slipping out, and I would immediately correct myself by saying, "I mean, I really like you," but I had messed that up pretty badly. I didn't want to be the first person to say I love you; I wanted him to say it first. "Boy, that liquid courage."

Almost every weekend, a few of our friends and family members would go out dancing. We would go to two different clubs, either the Stardust Lounge or French Quarters, and we would have a ball. Those were some good times, I tell you. I knew Matthew loved me because he showed it; he was a good provider and showed commitment. Everything was great, my life was on point, and I was very happy in my relationship with Matthew.

After Matthew and I moved in together, we lived together for two years. After we moved and Mitchel was born and my divorce was finalized, we decided to get married. Again, without expecting or receiving a proposal, I started planning our wedding. My first wedding was huge and expensive, and the planning lasted longer than the marriage itself, so we opted out of a large wedding. Matthew and I decided on February 14, 1999, to get married, which is Valentine's Day. We had also decided that we only wanted 50 of our closest relatives and friends to attend the wedding. We had a very small intimate wedding, and it only took me a month to plan it with a very small budget, and it was very lovely (*I'm smiling again*). I can say that when you know, you know.

Matthew started saying the words, "we're not going to remain living here for long." I've learned that when his wheels start turning, great things are going to happen, no matter what it is. When he says he's going to do something, it gets done; that's one of the things that I love about him—he is a man of his word.

In 1999 one day, we visited a good friend's townhouse, and I said to Matthew, "I want one of these." And well, you know what happened next; yes, Matthew and I went through the motions and we purchased a townhome in July of 1999, just five months after we got married. That was our first home together in Fremont, California, and I was so happy to have purchased our first home. Life was really shaped out for both of us.

We had plans, and we had goals. We were madly in love with each other; I would say that love was in full bloom. Matthew wasn't going to settle for living in the Townhouse very long. Not soon after moving there, I would say just over a year after living there, he asked me if I was ready to buy a bigger house, and I said yes. We went on the mission to find a house in various places in the Bay Area, and we couldn't find anything in our budget or that was worthy of us purchasing.

Do you remember my plan to move to Arizona that I mentioned earlier? Well, Matthews' wheels started turning again, and he asked me if I were serious about moving to Arizona, and I told him I was. Matthew and I visited Arizona in July of 1998.

We spent the 4th of July with one of my older sisters, and he too fell in love with Arizona—the freshness, how new it was, and how inexpensive it was.

That he remembered his visit and asked if I still wanted to move there, I was very happy. I began researching everything I could about Arizona, schools, daycares, jobs, shopping malls, and I learned a great deal about Arizona. During our visit with my sister, we looked at different types of homes and price ranges, so we had a pretty clear idea of what we wanted and what we were looking for in the lines of homes.

In 2001, we began mapping out our plan to move. We put our townhome on the market, sold it, and were off to Arizona. We moved to Arizona in August of 2001. It was very hard leaving family members behind, it was hard for me to leave my job of nine years behind, but I felt that our children would have a better life if they grew up in Arizona.

Matthew, the kids, and I have had a very lovely life; we were settling into Arizona nicely, and as I mentioned before, I was pretty content. During those times in early 2001, I really knew what it felt like to have all of your dreams come true and to really be happy in life. We both missed our families because we were very close to them, but we made it through. The kids were still young and I didn't hear them complain about anything. Having love in full bloom and living life was great.

The journey that I am on with Matthew continues to be great because this is something that we both have worked so hard for. I can't tell you that it's all easy, but what I can tell is that it is so worth it to have someone love me unconditionally, and the only thing that he ever asks for is to be appreciated.

One thing I have learned on my life journey about men is that for those that put 100% in their family, all they want is to be appreciated and not feel like a meal ticket. The same pastor that told me about divorce was the same pastor that told me about appreciating my husband. I am a strong believer that you find that just saying the words and meaning them, "I appreciate you," will make a difference in your marriage.

Sometimes, I just sit back and reflect on the journey that Matthew and I have traveled, and I remember the words I would always say to people about him, "I know that my husband loves me." Still, when I look back, I see that it wasn't enough for him to love me, I needed to love him the same way in return. Someone said to me that "Love isn't selfish," I said to that person, in my opinion, "it depends on what side of love you are looking at. I wouldn't want to give all the love that I could give to my mate and not reciprocate that back." So, in a sense, love could possibly be selfish, but it doesn't have to be when you have two hearts agreeing on one accord. I also believe that love between two people shouldn't be hard because if you love someone, you love them and the love should just flow. Have you heard the saying love shouldn't hurt? Well, think again, because quite the contrary, love does hurt sometimes, and that's my opinion, but I do believe that love will prevail.

To try to express to you the love that I have for my husband, the book isn't big enough, because over the years, through all our mishaps and mistakes, I know this is where I am supposed to be, with Matthew, he is my soulmate, the one God has chosen for me.

"Weeping may endureth for a night, but joy cometh in the morning."

Psalm 30:5

CHAPTER 7
TROUBLE IN PARADISE

This is a very sensitive chapter, and I want to handle it with care because it involves two other people that I love dearly, my husband and my oldest son and myself.

When I met Matthew, he didn't drink alcohol; he told me that he went through a 12-step program and didn't drink anymore. I left it at that. I started noticing changes in him just before our son was born in 1997, but I didn't say anything because we both were drinking and having a good time doing it. There were times when we lived in our second apartment that I would feel like he would overdrink. I just kept on with life because life was good and we were in the process of getting ready to move to Arizona, and I didn't want anything to get in the way of that.

Upon moving to Arizona, we both drank and I started seeing some patterns in both of us that were not healthy for the relationship. As my oldest son got older, he and Matthew would have disagreements all the time. I found myself in the middle of them, defending my son while trying to maintain a solid relationship with my husband. I tell you, the balancing act was very hard.

I felt like I needed to defend my son because he was just a kid, but I needed to be there for my husband as well. If you have never been in this situation, you have no idea what it's like trying to keep the peace between the two people you love. The more they disagreed, the more I interfered, and the more distant Matthew and I became.

A year later, in August of 2002, Matthew, the kids, and I flew back to California for my youngest sister's wedding. I am ashamed to tell you that I was pretty much drunk the entire wedding; it was a blur (*Thank God for Pictures*). The night of the wedding, I was so intoxicated, Matthew had to take care of the kids and me. However, I remember getting into the car to go home, and then I was out.

Matthew was not happy with me, and a few days later, Matthew asked me if he and I could talk. He explained how he felt about me drinking, and I heard him; he was right. As a mother and a wife, I should have been more cautious of how I was handling things. To this day, I am very conscious of my alcohol consumption; I control it, it doesn't control me.

I felt there was a problem with Matthew and Marcus, which went on for many years. In 2004, Matthew and Marcus had a very bad altercation, and I was so very upset, I called the police.

This was a very low point in our lives. I was caught between two people I love dearly, and I didn't know how to deal with this situation.

Matthew and I decided to separate; Matthew stayed with friends, and I stayed in the house with the children. We continued to work on our relationship, and I believe we were apart for just a few months, after which we decided to remain in the marriage, and Matthew came home.

Matthew and I just couldn't seem to find our rhythm, and two years later, we separated again. Still, it wasn't until 2011 that we had the biggest separation in our marriage. I can tell you that egos and alcohol played a huge part in the reason we were at odds and the reason we just didn't like each other anymore. We very much loved each other, but we just could not get it together. I felt that Matthew's drinking was now getting out of control, and I started voicing my opinion and wasn't going to put up with anything; I was mad. I can say for me that I was not having it. I finally found my voice and I was using it. I wasn't going to allow Matthew or anyone else to tell me what to do or how to do it. I meant business. I was a different person; I just didn't care anymore.

We verbally fought all the time. We didn't see eye to eye on anything. Furthermore, we talked badly to each other, and the relationship hit an all-time low. At this point, we decided that we were going to separate again, but this time the dreaded word "divorce" was mentioned.

"Here I go again," is all I could think about, another failed marriage. We had this big home we decided to buy and we couldn't find happiness in it. Our marriage was a mess, and I didn't know how to fix it. This separation wasn't like the other two. It was surreal and painful because we both were looking for homes to rent without each other, and all I could think of was the tremulous journey we were both on.

I was devastated and confused; how in the world did our relationship get here? Two people that were once madly in love were on a journey to disaster. Matthew found his house and I found mine; the kids came with me. Marcus was an adult and didn't need much supervision and our son Mitchel would go to his dad's house on the weekends while I would go out and party. I hit the streets, I partied, and I didn't care about anything that was going on. I was angry, bitter, hurt, and disgusted, all wrapped into one. My life at that point was in disarray, and I was so lost and broken. Mitchel was my rock at this time; he was all of 13 years old, seeing all of this.

When we moved out of the big house Matthew and I purchased and into a smaller house, Mitchel had a meltdown and said, "I want to go home!" That broke my heart because here I go again, going through a bad situation that involved my husband and me and I didn't sit the kids down to talk with them. I didn't consider their feelings, and I didn't learn anything from the last relationship.

I saw history repeating itself, and I couldn't deal with this, not again, not another divorce. Lord, Please Help Me!! Matthew and I were separated for two years. Our relationship was in jeopardy and I just didn't know how to fix it, repair it or change course at that point. Fortunately, Matthew never stopped looking after us; we settled on how much he would give me for Mitchel every month to help me. He would come over and do things for the kids and me and do things around my house.

Eventually, I got over my madness with time, and I would go to his house and stay with him and Mitchel. As I mentioned previously, Marcus was 21 years old during this time and he was doing him, living his life.

During the separation, I really thought that this would be the end of us. I decided to meet with my pastor and he told me to never say the word divorce. He said, as I mentioned earlier, "If you didn't hear

God say the word divorce, don't you mention it." At this time, I noticed that Matthew was making some changes and he stopped drinking alcohol, and he never drank again.

While I was out running the streets, partying, something strange happened. One day it was as if I was jolted, and it was at that moment I said, "I need to go back home and change this situation around," and I decided that I was going to make some changes. At that time, I didn't care about Matthew making any changes; I was focused on myself. I didn't watch any television or go out; I started praying, meditating, and journaling. I put all of my energy into Mitchel, focusing on me and being a life coach. I realized that I was broken, and I lost my way and myself in the shuffle of the separation.

I realized that in life as a married couple, we tuned up our cars, we got make-overs, and we made sure that we looked good, yet we went on year after year, and I never gave it one thought that what worked for Matthew me and in the late 1990s and early 2000s was no longer working in 2011. We let our marriage get into a rut; we didn't communicate anything we were feeling or any of our needs. We just argued and fought all the time.

Some women may not want to hear this, but I needed to find my place in my marriage. I learned a huge lesson on respect, and I wanted my husband back.

I needed to get back to what I knew and loved and that was with Matthew. Matthew and I decided that we loved each other and that neither of us wanted to get a divorce. I am a firm believer that if there is a spark of love left, God can turn it into a burning flame.

In 2013, we sat down and talked about our mistakes, how much we love each other and that we did not want to end our marriage. At that point, we decided to change the course of our journey and found a house, and we moved back in together. We weren't perfect, but I believe that we were perfect for each other. We both realize that there has to be respect in the marriage, and sometimes, you both have to regroup and start over afresh and that we did.

If I can be of some help to people who are planning on having a blended family, what I have experienced personally has taught me to be patient and talk to everyone involved. Please do not just move in together without checking in with the kids. Sometimes as adults, we don't consider the kids, as I mentioned before. They have feelings and opinions and need to be validated. Communication is key.

Note:

One thing that I must share with you is that although this was a tumultuous time in my marriage (this is probably the piece that I comment on the most when speaking with others about their relationship or relationships in general because, as I mentioned before, this was the worse time in my marriage), it also was the turning point. I always tell people how many times my husband and I separated and how I thought that we wouldn't make it, but we did, and that's the most important thing. It's okay to reminisce and think back on the past to see where you've both been and to measure where you are in the present but what I suggest to you as a couple is to always stay present in your marriage and do not allow the past to dictate your future goals.

Whatever flavor you add to your relationship to create the recipe that will keep it intact depends on the two of you. Just because there is trouble in the marriage doesn't mean that it has to end.

"A happy marriage is the union of two good forgivers."

-Ruth Bell Graham

CHAPTER 8
THEY DON'T KNOW ABOUT THIS HERE!

What some people don't know about Matthew and me is that we are in love. I believe our love for each other suffered short for a moment, but we never stopped loving each other. We have our disagreements, and we sometimes don't handle it perfectly, but we try our best not to go days and days without talking.

I have learned with my relationship that we need to communicate with each other because it is very important that we keep the lines of communication open at all times. As a wife, I know Matthews's patterns, when he's bothered by something, when he is upset about something, and when he's growing to a higher phase in life.

These are signs that, as his wife, I learned to recognize. Being tapped in and present in my marriage is one of the things that was missing in my first marriage and at the beginning of my current marriage. We are creatures of habit, and I believe that when the pattern and the course of the journey change, that's a red flag that should be addressed. Checking in with my husband to see how he's doing, making sure he's okay and not distracted by foolishness is exactly what I do. (Are you alright? Is everything okay? What's going with you today?) These are the questions I ask Matthew on a regular basis.

People think they know us; they may know a little bit of what went on in our marriage because they were there when we were going through it, but they don't know how strong the bond is between Matthew and me. We fought for our marriage and didn't allow any outside influences to distract us.

He and I have learned that our past doesn't define who we are today; we don't let the past dictate our future plans together as a couple. I love my family; I love my children, but my marriage comes first. I can say now that my children are grown and both have their own relationships, that they, too, have to find their way in it.

Only God can infiltrate what we have. Claiming and naming is what I do, "My Marriage Is a Successful Marriage," because that's how I see it. We've gone through hell and back, and we are still standing and are on course for our journey.

I believe that only you and your spouse can define the type of marriage you want to have—whether learning how to be present, showing up every day, taking care of each other no matter what. God, Marriage, and Children, in that order, I know I am going to get some pushback on this, but you go to Genesis 2:24, and there it is written. *"Therefore, shall a man leave his father and his mother, and shall cleave unto his wife: and they shall be one flesh."*

I am very careful with who I share my personal information. I don't confide in people who have never been married or who are bitter after their marriage has ended. My sex life is off-limits to everyone except Matthew; I cherish my marriage, and I don't play with my husband. What I mean by that is I don't take too kindly to other women trying to get my husband's attention, and let me make this very clear, "I will not share my husband with another woman; that isn't going to happen."

Marriage isn't for the faint at heart, it is serious business, and I look at it as an investment that both he and I have worked very hard to sustain. Over the years, I've learned that all Matthew wants is to be appreciated; he never asks for anything. I always joke that it is very hard to shop for him because he doesn't ask for anything. On the other hand, I have the "I want" really bad.

I can proudly say today that the relationship with Matthew and Marcus is very good, Mitchel is doing well, and I love my family. The lessons I have learned throughout the years have brought us where we are today. Every day isn't sunshine and kisses, but it is damn good. I have everything I need—I am grateful for my husband, and I am content in my marriage.

You, too, can have a successful marriage if that's what you want. I try not to talk bad about my husband to other people because I believe that the way I see my husband is how others will see him. I try my best to let Matthew know that I love him by showing it and telling him how much I love him. Matthew and I are at a stage in our life where we are on a mission to live a long, healthy, fulfilled life together, and we are here for each other. We are very selective about who we allow into our lives.

Matthew and I share a lot of common interests, which I feel are very important in a marriage. He's not hanging out with the men and I'm not out with the women. We are home together, he's on one end of the couch and I am on the other end enjoying movies and enjoying our time together. We look forward to things to do as a couple, and we look for couples for our friends.

A funny story I will share with you. I remember around the year 2010; I was very frustrated with

Matthew because I felt like he had given up on our marriage because he didn't want to go anywhere. He didn't want to do anything, and I went to the hair shop and was explaining to my hairdresser how I felt about him, and she had to stop doing my hair and said to me, "Let me get this straight, Matthew is at home, correct? And you are upset about that? You know exactly where your husband is, and you are upset?" She went on to say to me, "Don't you know that there are women who don't know where their husbands are, and yours is at home and you are complaining?" Boy, that was an eye-opener for me.

I am a living witness that marriage is not easy by any means, but it's just like anything else in life you have or want, you have to fight for it. You put in the work no matter what comes. I know how easy it is to throw in the towel and say the famous saying, "I'm Done."

I am a living witness that if you both make the necessary changes, you know about that tiny spark. (*I'm excited now, I'm stirred up now".*)

Here's something else you probably won't believe, but the very people smiling in your face are the very people who are not happy about your marriage succeeding. Some people don't want to see you and your spouse come up (together); word to the wise, be careful who you let into your marriage circle. I'm not saying that you can't have your friends, but I am saying, always take care of yourself and your mate first and foremost.

Let me address the 50/50 rule in my marriage. Although I think that it is realistic, I don't live by that rule. There are days where I can only give 30 percent. Matthew will show up pulling that 70 percent because he knows me; he knows my patterns. He knows how passionate I am about everything in my life. Some would call me emotional; you can call me what you like, but I call it "I care." Therefore, he knows when he gets that phone call, he jumps right in 70 percent in tow, "What's wrong." We rarely have 50/50 situations, but we do our best to be supportive of one another and be there in time of need.

Once we found our rhythm in our marriage and were on the same page, on the same path on our journey, love and life just flowed. It feels so smooth, and when we go through rough patches, we are able to sustain them and bounce back. I keep the words in my thoughts, the vows that we both took, "for better or for worse, for richer or poor, for sickness and in health until the marriage runs its course.

We can't run away at every sign of hardship. Like Matthews says, "You can't have the good without the bad." Don't change directions because of obstacles you may face. I realized that when we made it through the bad, the good was smooth sailing.

Ladies, a man has to be a man, and what I mean by that is, don't disrespect your husband and talk down to him. He is supposed to be your king, your protector, and from my experience with my husband, I stand with him and we make decisions together. It wasn't always like that, but as the head of the family, my husband appreciates when we talk about our plan together. I let him know some of my desires and he lets me know his.

I don't go to my husband saying, "this is what I am doing." I ask him, "what do you think if I did this?" Both our input matters. I don't use "I, Me," it's always "We, Us, Ours"; this is the language that we use. And if it isn't used, we will correct each other.

Men, appreciate your woman, she should be your queen, and you should only have eyes for her. You'll be surprised how many other women are looking to see just how tight the bond is between the two of you and if you flinch, they got you.

Matthew and I are still learning how to agree to disagree. In our marriage, we are constantly growing, but we strive to grow together as a couple.

Something that I am so grateful for is how attentive Matthew is to me. He makes sure that I am well taken care of; he's also a funny guy, and he makes me laugh without him even knowing that he is doing so. I like how he calls himself not interested in the shows that I watch but somehow finds himself always sitting on the couch watching them with me and chiming in on every aspect of the show that I have to literally pause the show. At first, I am a little annoyed, but then we get into a deep conversation about what is going on with the character's on "Love and Hip," and what was meant for entertainment has now turned into a couple's counseling session, LOL! These are the moments that I cherish with him. When I think about how we spend our time together, it's nothing fancy; it's just us being us and being together. I can go into the game room or the office to watch television, but Matthew won't have that; he will give up the television so that I can stay in the same room with him. It's not about what we do when we are together but how we do it; we just want to be together with each other. I believe that finding your rhythm in your marriage is like harmony, so to speak; it's the small things that matter the most. I appreciate it when we are out in public and Matthew reaches for my hand all the time, and we walk hand in hand. He makes sure that he opens the store doors for me, although we're going to have to work on him opening the car door, LOL! However, I feel that it is very important that every couple carve out some fun time with their mate.

Both Matthew and I are lovers of music, and he can play music for hours on end, and while he's playing the music, I'm dancing. Sometimes he plays music while I'm trying to watch TV that I have to turn the television up very loud to send a message to him to turn down the music, and he'll say, "Oh, I guess that's my cue to turn the music off, LOL!" As I mentioned, we both can listen to music for hours; this is how we spend some of our quality time together. We take bike rides together, we work out together, we swim together. I'm not a fan of cooking, but we also cook together all the time, especially for the holidays, we are both in the kitchen putting it down.

My family calls Matthew "Inspector Gadget" because he knows a lot about so much, he has so much wisdom that I have to stop and ask him sometimes, "How do you know that?" I call him "Mr. Know it all." LOL! And there isn't anything that he can't fix; he's just that awesome. Here's a suggestion, maybe as a couple, when the two of you have some downtime, the two of you could sit down together and just write down all the special things that you love about each other, make a game of it and share with each other. I think it's important that you tell each other good things about one another. Both Matthew and I learned how not to be so serious but laugh and enjoy each other.

Find your recipe as I've mentioned or you can create new ones if you have to, but put the work into it and keep it fresh. You rarely see Matthew without Carol, we share a bond that is unexplainable, and we both want this union to work, and I give all credit to God.

We know that every marriage is different; what works in my marriage may not work for you in your marriage. Only Matthew and I can define the type of marriage we want to have. As I mentioned, I'm not very fond of cooking. I know how to cook, but I really don't like cooking. I have three sisters who cook every night for their spouses, and I know people who have shared that their husbands don't like leftovers. Only you can define the type of marriage you want to have and the course or journey you two will go down.

I said all of that to say this, you too can have a long healthy, successful marriage. I tell you this "They Don't Know About This Here! This right here, we fought for this, and this is my recipe for my successful marriage.

"A successful marriage isn't the union of two perfect people, it's that of two imperfect people who have learned the value of forgiveness and grace."

-Darlene Schacht

CHAPTER 9
WHAT MAKES A MARRIAGE/RELATIONSHIP SUCCESSFUL?

THOUGHTS FROM OTHER COUPLES

I feel like I can speak on this because I am in my second marriage, and I have a lot of experience with 22 years in. It hasn't always been flowers and kisses, believe me, but the bad, along with greater times, has brought us where we are today. Marriage is the biggest investment I have made in my life, along with having my children. Marriage isn't for the lightweight, fly-by-the-seat-of-your-pants people; it's a real investment and should be treated as such.

I saw some marriages run their course because one of the partners wasn't fully vested in the marriage; hence, the breakdown. I believe that marriage is sacred and very serious and should be cherished. I want my husband to never have to worry about another man coming into our marriage and this is how he makes me feel pertaining to other women.

My husband, helpmate, right hand, and ride-or-die makes me feel safe and secure at all times. Being the humans we are, we sometimes fall short because no one is perfect. This is where the trust and communication in my marriage come into play. I have learned how to play the hand that is dealt to me. There were times when we both came to a fork in the road and had to ask ourselves, "should I stay or should I leave," that was a huge decision we made together to stick it out and fight for our marriage; this is our marriage, our investment, our recipe.

We talked about it and decided with help from God that we didn't want to end our marriage. I mentioned that a pastor asked me if I heard God say, "get a divorce." Those words prompted me to rethink things and fight for my marriage.

In my belief, every marriage is different with different struggles, and some will make it and some will not. Still, whatever each couple decides to do, it will take two working together for the greater good. I am a living witness, and I keep repeating that if there is a spark of love left, with both willing, hard work, faith, and prayer, God can ignite a burning flame. He did it for my marriage. Don't give up on your relationship; fight for it, talk it out, work it out.

In my opinion, wedding vows are not taken seriously. I am not sure if some couples pay attention to what they say when they say their vows because, most of the time, the vows aren't honored. Some couples are so excited about the thought of being married or the celebration that comes with having a wedding that they rush to the altar and the vows are pushed to the side.

I'm simply saying that you can have a long successful marriage if that is what the two of you are striving for. We all have different definitions of what makes a marriage a success or what makes it work and why some last for years and some run their course.

Here are a few couples who shared their journeys and what makes their marriages a success.

Couple #1 thoughts

1. How long have you and your husband been married? (Elaborate)

My husband and I have been married 23 years and six months. On May 16, 2022, we will have been married 24 years. However, we have been together for 25 years. We've been together for over half of our lifetime. We got engaged at the age of 19 and 21 and married at 20 and 22.

2. What was the dating process like for you and your husband?

We had a long-distance relationship, as he lived in Florida and I lived in California. So, our relationship was not physical but more emotional. We became best friends before lovers. We talked about everything from our dreams and ambitions to where we saw each other in the next two, five, ten years. When we realized we were on the same wavelength, we both knew we had found our soulmate.

3. How long did you two date before he proposed marriage?

We dated for one year and nine months before he proposed to me. He told me I was his wife on day two of our meeting, and I initially thought he was just joking as he didn't know me. But as time went on, I too realized I had found my person.

After asking my stepfather and mother for their permission, he officially proposed to me on a trip to California. We were at the Pepper Mill in Sacramento, California, and after dinner, he said, "From the day I met you, I knew God sent you to me, as I was in that meeting seeking him, but when I saw you, I knew you were my wife my Queen, will you do me the honor of being my wife?" It was him, my sister (Monica), and myself; in tears, I gladly said, "yes, my king," and accepted his ring.

Many years later, sitting on a beach in Jamaica, he looked over at me and said, "I said you were going to be my wife, and look at you sitting on this beautiful beach enjoying life with me. Now, who is the joke on... lol."

4. What did the proposal mean to you, and do you think that it is an important part?

The proposal was a nice gesture and I appreciate all the steps that led to his proposal. He was such a gentleman and a bit old fashion. Though I enjoyed being proposed to, what was important to me was us living in the same state and having the ability to see and be together daily.

5. How do you define a successful marriage? What does that look like to you and your husband?

A successful marriage means open and honest communication, being best friends, and a team. We look out for each other. We celebrate each other's success and wins and make sure we keep each other progressing forward by encouraging and uplifting one another. We are each other's biggest cheerleaders. A win for him or myself is a win for us. Our marriage is deeper than being in love, as you can fall in and out of love several times during the marriage. We value the commitment, the friendship, and our family dynamic, and as a result, the love flows. We are team D&A as there is no D without A. D&A for life...

Couple #2 thoughts

1. How long have you and your husband been married? (Elaborate)

My husband and I have been married for 19 years but actually together for a total of 26 years. We met at a club where neither of us was looking for anything serious, but fate saw differently.

2. Did your husband propose to you? If yes, please do tell me; if not, how did or do that make you feel today?

My husband did not propose traditionally. We dated for seven years, and of those seven, we lived together for about four years. Within those seven years, we had so much FUN! We traveled a lot and basically learned about each other in so many ways that others fail to explore by rushing into a lifelong commitment.

After seven years of dating, I needed more. More of a defined commitment other than dating, so I asked my husband what his plans were. From that question, his exact words were, "If you want to get married, I'll marry you. Pick a date." Very romantic, huh? I want a true proposal! Being married is great because I'm not navigating life on my own. However, getting to where we are to today wasn't always easy. We've had amazing times and some turbulent times. But getting through them made the marriage stronger. One great thing that my husband said to me before we got married was that divorce was not an option. I thank him for that because there have been times when I wanted to throw in the towel.

3. How do you and your husband communicate during a conflict?

During a conflict, we're both very vocal about what's displeasing. Sometimes we don't see eye to eye, but at least the concern has been presented as something we need to work on. Sometimes giving examples can help with understanding as well.

4. Please tell me about what you and your husband do together every day as a couple. (Prayer each day) so important.

My husband and I pray EVERY DAY. God is the head of our household where we reverence Him in everything we do. We also often communicate throughout the day to just check in, shoot the breeze and see how each other day is going.

5. What does a successful marriage look like to you and your husband?

A successful marriage is putting God first in everything. Once we align with God and his word, everything falls into place. Taking marriage vows is a serious thing. So, as a couple, we try to approach everything as a union.

Couple #3 thoughts

1. How long have you been married?

43 years

2. What are your thoughts on Red Flags, and how should they be handled/addressed in a relationship?

Red flag is a term used in fraud investigations, indicating that a process control may not be working. The red flag, if significant and combined with other red flags, should be investigated and corrective action taken. I think that they should handle similarly in relationships.

3. Define compromise in a marriage.

Compromise is the result of negotiations, where parties have common as well as conflicting interests or needs. A good compromise results in both parties getting their important needs met, and the terms of the compromise result in increased trust and a long-term relationship.

4. What made your marriage successful for so many years?

Love, i.e., looking out for the best interest of the other person and knowing that the other person is doing the same. Forgiveness, i.e., one party not holding a grudge when wronged, and the other party makes a sincere intent to never again make that same or a similar mistake. Commitment over time is important. Help from God is huge.

Couple # 4 thoughts

1. How long have you and your husband been married? (Elaborate)

We've been married 22 years. We dated for one year and were engaged for one year.

2. What was the dating process like for you and your husband?

The dating process was wonderful in that it was a time of discovery. By that, I mean we both pretty much knew what we wanted by that stage of our lives. We married 'later' 40/42 respectively and had both traveled quite a bit. We lived lives that were full in terms of career and relationships. My husband is Nigerian. Although he had been in the US for over 20 years by the time we met (college and career), he still maintained close home ties. Because of my previous travels and being open to other cultures, getting to know him, his family and friends was a lovely experience, and so was him getting to know mine. He was very much at ease with meeting new people, which impressed me. His friends were great, and it became apparent that our 'circles of influence' were solid. We both love jazz, spicy foods, dancing, taking naps (believe it or not - LOL), and exploring ideas. Of course, there were a few bumps in the road, but we tended to align on the most important issues. I was impressed with his transparency —he wanted me to know who he is and what he values. Between the two of us, I must say that initially, I was the more guarded one.

3. How long did you two date before he popped the question? What did the proposal mean to you, and do you think it is an important part?

We had dated for a year before he proposed. Unknown to me, he went to my mom and stepdad to ask their permission (yes, even though we were more 'mature'), then he went to my mentor, who was extremely influential in my life and talked to him. He plotted with the owner of the most expensive restaurant in the city, and after dinner, they brought out this HUGE balloon with a teddy bear inside holding a note that read, "I love you; will you marry me?" Everyone in the restaurant seemed to be in on it, but it was great. Then he had arranged for my parents to meet us at a jazz club afterward to toast and celebrate. The esteem, consideration and respect he showed to those closest to me was most meaningful. He values familial relationships because he understands that the future involves everyone on both sides, not just the two of us.

On our wedding day, during a toast, his friend said that the night he and I met, he called him at 2:00 in the morning. Of course, he thought something was wrong. "What's wrong, man? Are you alright?" he asked. My husband (to be) said, "I think I just met the one!" I didn't know that until our wedding day! (Cue the tears)

4. How do you define a successful marriage? What does that look like to you and your husband?

When we were dating, he asked me if I believed in God and said attending church is very important to him. He said that if we're to be married, God has to be at the center of our lives, like a pyramid with God at the apex. We came together on that as even though

I had been away from the church for many years, I'm a believer. I was open to returning, and I'm so glad I did. Now I won't say that this is the standard way of evangelizing, but we HAVE been active in our faith ever since.

Faith, respect, love, humor, family, all of these things, are critically important, but what's also critical is defining what that MEANS to each other. What does that look like? 'Faith' to one person may mean never stepping into a church but regularly communing with nature, 'Humor' may mean all the raunchiest stuff you can find to one person, but to the other only rom-com. 'Family' may mean only a tight circle to one, and to another a huge tent and an ever-expanding 'tribe.'

What are their goals, dreams and financial & health habits? Not sexy, but very important.

Learning a person's 'love language' makes for a smoother life together, i.e., does one person love to receive gifts and tokens of appreciation, while the other believes that doing things around the house is an expression of love and so never thinks to give a gift? Does one love physical touch/displays of affection or needs words of appreciation or encouragement on a regular basis? You don't have to 'interview' the person to find out, but pay attention, and you'll learn.

I also believe that developing friendships with

couples who have been married longer than you make for a rich experience. It's not that they're necessarily 'counselors,' but they provide us with great examples. We have friends who have been married 30, 40, 50 years, and they are great because of their life experience and humor. It also gives us a view into the 'arc of life.' In case you're wondering, we also have young married couples and single friends; we don't discriminate and hope we can be helpful to them as well.

"I love you with all my heart, to have forever-never to part. This is a promise engrained in me, take my hand and let it be."

-Diana Lynn

Chapter 10
Contentment - A State of Happiness and Satisfaction

My Love Letter To Matthew

Dear Matthew:

I never thought that meeting you 26 years ago would have led to the journey we are on now. We have stood the test of time; I can truly say that we have been through hell and back again.

We've weathered three separations, one almost leading to divorce but here we stand. I have never ever questioned your love for me; you have always shown me the love that a wife deserves in a marriage. I need you to know that I love you more than words can express, and I appreciate how you stepped up to the plate and became a stepfather to Marcus and how you make sure that your family is always taken care of.

You are my everything, the man that I am in love with, and I am thanking God that I can spend the rest of my life with someone that I can trust, depend on and honor. You are my best friend. Although we've been together for many years, we are still learning how to make sure that we are available for each other.

I am very content and happy in my marriage, and it is partly because of you taking good care of me. You are my rock, my right arm, my helpmate, and my lover. Thank you for showing up every day to show me that you have my back no matter what.

Sometimes I watch you while you sleep, knowing how tired you are, but there isn't anything that I ask you for that you do not provide. You'll keep going in order to please me, and I recognize that.

There are not enough words to tell you that I love you beyond the moon and back, and there is no other person that I would rather be on this successful journey with.

Love your wife, Carol!

"Winning Takes Precedence Over All.

There's No Gray Area. No Almost"

-Kobe Bryant

CHAPTER 11
WHAT WINNING LOOKS LIKE

I believe with all my heart that every couple starts out wanting to have a successful marriage. However, a one-sided marriage will never work. It requires showing value and working together no matter what comes your way as a couple, seeing the good while not pointing out only the other person's faults or shortcomings, and standing in the gap for your mate when that person can't bring much to the table for whatever reason. A successful marriage involves being present and attentive to each other's needs and having each other's backs while being able to tell that person, although not in a judgmental way, that they were wrong in a situation not pertaining to the marriage.

When situations in the marriage pertain to money arise, this is a huge deal-breaker for some couples. It doesn't matter who brings home the most money or whether you have joint bank accounts or separate bank accounts, as the two of you can figure that out. What matters is that whatever the conflict is in the relationship, it is being taken care of. My husband and I used to have money issues, but we've worked them out; still, remember that what once worked may not continue to work, as I stated before, and this is where communication comes in. Marriage is a union, not "I, Me, My," but should be "Ours, Us, We." So, what if she makes more money? Then she can contribute more than him or vice versa. You both are winning because you are a team, and that's what teammates do—they "share and bear" to keep the marriage afloat by any means necessary.

I know you all know the saying, "what is mine, is his, and what is his is mine"; if you want to win at this thing called marriage, you shouldn't be selfish; you should be working for the betterment of the marriage. Winners never quit; they move forward in spite of any situation that may arise because of the love they share. Winners don't allow outside distractions to deter them; they include the other person in all the moves they make, no matter what. Your partner should know your whereabouts; "who goes somewhere without letting their mate know?" All of this is my belief that helped me and my husband have a successful marriage. I don't call it keeping tabs; I call it knowing where your partner is and not having to worry about them because they were courteous enough to let you know what they are doing and when they are doing it. Respecting the other person is vital as I can't see any relationship lasting without respect for the other person. A couple can be in a relationship like that, but what type of relationship would that be at that point?

Create your recipe for what you want your relationship to look like, feel like, or be like. God, Love, Trust, Honor, Faith, Prayer, Patience, Respect and Commitment is the recipe that I used to help make my marriage a success. Some couples may need more intimacy, more quality time spent together, conversations or more attention paid to them or whatever it takes; only the two of you can determine that. Don't be afraid to try and create the relationship you desire. As I mentioned earlier, I believe that communication is the key to every relationship.

Here are a few things (*ingredients*) that I believe will help a relationship be a winner. I've learned that incorporating God first or a higher being in your relationship is a plus; it's a way to go when times get tough and they will. Love is very important to have between two people in a relationship or marriage as without it, why bother? You know the saying, "Patience is a virtue," and it is one quality that both must possess to be able to sustain a solid, productive relationship. Trust will put the both of you at ease, knowing that you don't have to worry about the other doing anything unnecessary. Without trust, the foundation of the relationship will most likely not succeed and fail. Honor simply means valuing the relationship with the greatest respect there is; having honor means that the relationship is solid. Respect in a relationship shows that you care about how the other person feels and it will help keep both of you moving in the same directions. Faith, you only need just a small bit of it; as you know, it is believing in the relationship and knowing that it cannot and will not fail. Commitment is vowing to be all in, 100% vested into the relationship or marriage without hesitation. Lastly, but surely not least, is prayer; if you believe in prayer, you should already know how it works. Prayer changes situations while waiting with patience and having faith and love. Prayer can be a relationship saver. Believe me, I know this all too well.

What worked for my marriage is, putting God first, and along with prayer and faith, you have an awesome recipe for greatness and success. Working together, crying together, praying together, laughing together, not giving up on each other when things get tough, strengthening the bond between the two of you by communication and listening to solve conflict is what winning looks like. If you can, always see the value in your marriage and put it first before family or friends. Don't leave your partner alone to figure things out; jump in and be that helpmate they need, that shoulder to cry on, the support system that is solid and loyal. I always say, "Loyalty" is huge, and it is very important in any type of relationship, and in a marriage, it is very important.

Some people might not believe me when I say that I go hard for my marriage; I have invested so many years into it that there's no turning back now. I probably mentioned before that I know that Matthew and I drive each other crazy, but at the end of the day when I see how hard he rides for our family and me, that's what winning looks like. When there are hard times and the both of you just keep moving in the right direction together and look up and there's the sunlight shining through, that's what winning looks like.

Sometimes in a relationship, the finances aren't looking too good, but you both sit down and talk about, pray about it, and map out a plan, and then the next thing you know, the finances start shaping up, and you're able to keep moving, that's what winning looks like.

When our children are in need of anything, I don't care how upset we are with them, Matthew and I are always showing up together to help them; he never leaves me alone to solve any problems by myself. Winning is working together not only when things are going well but when there are hard times, that's when you have to work the hardest but don't stop.

Create your own recipe for success so that you, too, can be winners. Blessing!

"She Believed She Could, So She Did"

-R.S. Grey

About the Author

Carol F. Kirkendoll

Carol F. Kirkendoll was born and raised in the Bay Area, San Francisco, California. She is a very spiritual person who loves to motivate and encourage others. She holds both a Bachelor's and an Associate's degree in Healthcare Administration, and she is a Certified Life Coach with a life coaching business, CORE Life Coaching, LLC.

Carol has been in the medical field for 31 years, and for 14 of those years, she has worked as an educator. Her passion is to always help others to see value in themselves and build their self-esteem. Everything that Carol does in her life, she is greatly passionate about.

"He who dwells in the secret place of the most high shall abide under the shadow of the almighty."

Psalms 91:1

AFTER-THOUGHTS

After reflecting on everything that my husband and I went through, I really started thinking about my children and how all of this may have affected them. This is my story and my beliefs and the real-life events that we all went through, but when I look at the four of us now, we are all doing well today. I pride myself on being the best wife and mother that I can be, and I always think of "Greater, Later," greater things to come, and that is exactly what has happened to me. I have a loving husband, two great sons, and these three people I love more than life itself. I serve a God that is so powerful and merciful and he provides endless blessings every day. I am not religious, but I am a very spiritual person who loves God greatly.

I have a love for human life, which makes me love people in general. I love helping people and motivating them, as this brings me so much joy. I can't express the feeling that I have inside when I know that I have made a difference in someone's life. I've been told many times that I can't save the world, but I always say, if I can touch one person, then I feel that I have done my part. I was a little hesitant to put my story out there for the world to see, but I feel that someone needs to hear this, and my hope is that this book will help encourage someone in some way.

What do you know now about you and your relationship that you didn't know before reading my book?

What can you do in your current relationship to see more value?

How will you handle conflict when it presents itself?

Will you consider therapy if ever needed?

What does a successful marriage look like to you?